A TINY BOOK ABOUT GRATITUDE

A SIMPLE PRACTICE WITH SUPERPOWER STRENGTH

Heather Tobin

Rock Your Mud

Newmarket, Ontario, Canada

Copyright © 2020 by Heather Tobin.

All rights reserved. No part of this publication may be reproduced, distributed or transmitted in any form or by any means, including photocopying, recording, or other electronic or mechanical methods, without the prior written permission of the publisher, except in the case of brief quotations embodied in critical reviews and certain other noncommercial uses permitted by copyright law.

Heather Tobin/Rock Your Mud

A Tiny Book About Gratitude/Heather Tobin —1st ed.

ISBN 978-1-7774410-0-5

Dedicated to you, dear reader.

CONTENTS

INTRODUCTION..7

CHAPTER ONE - The List.................................11

CHAPTER TWO - Surprise Gratitude Reminders...........15

CHAPTER THREE - Gratitude for Challenging Times..17

CHAPTER FOUR - Gratitude in Motion (On the Go)....23

CHAPTER FIVE - Prompts and Ideas............................25

CHAPTER SIX - Gratitude - It's in You to Feel...................29

CHAPTER SEVEN - Gratitude for the Future.................31

SOME CLOSING THOUGHTS..35

ACKNOWLEDGEMENTS...37

ABOUT THE AUTHOR 39

CONNECTIONS..41

ADDITIONAL GRATITUDE PAGES...............43

INTRODUCTION

I consider this book the beginning. It is the start of my publishing journey, but more importantly, practicing gratitude was the beginning of how I got to where I am today.

My intention is that this simple book acts as a palate cleanser. Something we could all use regularly, but especially during the extraordinary situation that we currently find ourselves in here in 2020. Wow, just saying that feels so futuristic. Wasn't it 1995 yesterday?

Gratitude is a way of exploring life through a positive lens. If you already have a practice, I invite you to deepen it or experience it differently with the ideas shared here. If you've never had a gratitude practice, I want to start by letting you know that it took me a few years before this on-again-off-again relationship became a commitment. I didn't realize it at the time, but gratitude was going to become the foundation upon which I rebuilt my life.

Are you at a turning point in your life and not sure which way to go? Perhaps you feel stuck, depleted or hopeless? Maybe you feel good and you want to feel even better? Whatever it might be, there is a place for gratitude.

In my late 20s, I found myself at a crossroads. How my life was playing out was no longer enjoyable to me. I didn't feel I had a purpose. I didn't understand the point of life and often felt lost, confused and empty. I was about a decade into my anxiety and depression chapters. I remember the moment of being taken to the hospital by ambulance from high school with what I'd later learn was an anxiety attack. Grade 10 was not a good year. A few years later, I would be medicated for generalized anxiety disorder; a couple years after that, I'd quit the meds cold turkey and spiral into one of the most trying times of my life.

Through a series of equally messy and beautiful events in my 20s - going back to school while working full-time, meeting several practitioners who worked with a variety of holistic healing methods and learning about all sorts of personal development practices – without knowing it, I would bring everything together during the final session of my Codependency Support Group. It all came down to eating popcorn watching the movie "The Secret."

At the time, and even now, I still know many people who scoff at the concepts and teachings shared in that movie. Guess what? So did I. I thought it was an absolute laughable pile of rubbish. I did not believe that I could create a life worth living by having a few mindset shifts and starting a gratitude practice.

But, as the Divine would have it, a year or so after watching that movie, something clicked. I haven't the slightest idea what it was, but it was enough to make me start a regular gratitude practice. Quite honestly, I didn't quite grasp why I was doing it; I just sat down at some point every day and would write down everything I was grateful for in that moment. It brought me a strange sense of comfort. On my most challenging days, sometimes all I could be grateful for was the journal I was writing in and that the pen worked. Sometimes I was even grateful for cuss words and how I was able to use them as 'sentence enhancers' to express the challenging highlights of my day.

Having a gratitude practice was therapeutic and cathartic. It was also free, which was an added bonus since I was spiritually, emotionally and financially bankrupt at the time.

Fast forward a bunch of years: an opportunity presented itself for me to take some time to write this tiny book about Gratitude. It's a topic that I speak on endlessly with clients and whoever will listen. As an Intuitive Healer, Spiritual Life Guide and Medium, people often ask me what they can do to feel better. After the typical basic suggestions of sleep, nutrition and movement, gratitude is next on the list. Wait, no, that's not right. Gratitude is *first* on the list.

What I would love for you to know is that had it not been for a gratitude practice, I would not be where I am today. It has taken me years of continuous commitment and devotion to arrive at this place in my life journey.

In the following pages, I've created some practical exercises that I teach and have used myself. My goal is to help you think of gratitude as a way of being and seeing life in a certain way. My intention is to also invite you to consider some creative ways of doing your practice so that you can experience gratitude in a whole new way.

Although it took quite some time for me to cement this practice into my day-to-day life, I can't imagine my days without it now. Good days, bad days and all the days in between - gratitude is with me like a loyal companion. It may serve you well to keep in mind that a gratitude practice is somewhat like learning a new language in that it takes time and effort. We are conditioned and trained to see and experience so much negativity in the world, that this new way of being and seeing might feel very strange to us. This is completely normal. Keep going.

I hope you find something in these pages that you like and that you'll let your own gratitude practice stick around long enough for the magic to happen.

The beginning.

CHAPTER ONE

The List

Let's talk a little about the most commonly known gratitude practice. The list! Fancy, right? If you're not comfortable with writing in this book (trust me - it's taken me decades to get comfortable with highlighting and writing in books), this is the part where I encourage you to find yourself a nice little journal or notebook to use instead.

If you're a stationery aficionado like me, choosing the journal or notebook is possibly the hardest part, but try not to let perfection delay you too much.

Now that you have your favourite notebook and trusty writing instrument ready to go, you can write your gratitude list. A typical best practice is to have a set time at some point each day that suits you to begin working your gratitude muscle.

It may be helpful to pair this practice with something else you do each day, like waiting for the kettle to boil or the moment after that first sip of coffee before you dress and dash out the door. Or maybe it's what you do before you get out of bed in the morning because you keep your journal and pen right there on your nightstand. (Pro tip!)

Some people like mornings because it helps set the tone for the day ahead; others prefer night as a way to wrap up the day.

When I started my practice I was a night writer, but what I noticed is that sometimes it felt a little obligatory. Although it was a good habit, it was almost an auto-pilot thing and I wasn't really feeling the depth of gratitude I once did.

I wanted to consider additional ways to engage in gratitude that went beyond the page. I wanted to keep things fresh and new as we can easily become complacent and sometimes bored with our rituals. This can lead to stopping altogether, especially if we aren't achieving the desired result or noticing a change in how we are feeling.

The aim of gratitude is not to 'get' anything though. The intention is to appreciate all that we currently have, help us maintain a positive mindset, find the silver lining during the storms and allow ourselves a bit of a reprieve from coasting through our days in a way that is more connected.

I think we all have moments or periods in our life that feel as if they have whizzed by and we haven't given them enough appreciation for time well spent. Take a moment to jot down a few things that you're grateful for today in your notebook or in the space provided.

CHAPTER TWO

Surprise Gratitude Reminders

This is one of my favourite gratitude exercises! It's a way of sprinkling gratitude throughout your day via the route of surprise.

You can set an alarm or notification on your phone at a random time and when you hear it, you'll think, write or say anything in that moment you're grateful for. Yep, even if you're standing in a shop picking up a coffee. I'm sure the barista would love some appreciation.

One of the reasons I like this activity so much is because it provides an opportunity for us to get into the present, centered and zero in on Gratitude, if only for a moment.

Another extra surprise option is sticky-note style. The idea is that you place them in various places around your space. The bathroom mirror, inside a cabinet, your wallet, inside the fridge on your lunch. A simple prompt that says 'I am grateful for….' ought to do the trick. Or you could think of a few things you're grateful for, write them down and hide these longer notes.

You could even write down something you're grateful for about yourself. I guarantee that when you see that little gratitude love note to self you'll smile and may feel just a hint of the warm and fuzzies. I know, I know, just try it!

For bonus points, stick a few in random books that are in your 'to read' pile; you'll find them when you least expect it. When you find them again, you'll be reminded in the moment of those original notes you jotted down. Be sure to include the dates on these ones too; I've had folks come back many months later and say 'hey, look what I found!' It made us both feel pretty awesome.

* * *

Speaking of surprises!

Now might be a good time to introduce you to a little thing I've had on the go for a few years now.

The online Gratitude Community is a place where you can meet like-souled folks and engage in a daily gratitude practice. Each day there is a gratitude reminder prompt and folks share what they are grateful for.

The Gratitude Community is a space to fill your cup.

Overall, the space is ideal for people who are interested in personal and spiritual development and all things magical mindset.

If you're ready to join us, head over to

www.heathertobin.ca/connection

CHAPTER THREE

Gratitude for Challenging Times

At the time of writing this, we are neck-deep in the year 2020. To say that things are challenging to some degree or another for just about everyone feels like an understatement. It's times like these that make me sit back and think of everything, big and small, that needs appreciation. How on earth could it be possible to find gratitude when it feels like the world, or even your personal world, is falling apart?

One of the questions I often get is 'how do I begin a gratitude practice?' The second most asked question is 'how do I have a gratitude practice when things feel particularly challenging and difficult?'

It took me a long time and many years working on myself to see that there really could be gratitude for every moment. Not always 'in' the moment, but eventually. It came down to a lot of intentional choosing and conscious thought, which wasn't always easy.

I see gratitude as an opportunity to be a palate cleanser. Something to help us clear our mind and energy field.

This is not meant to say the pain isn't there, discredit feelings around tough circumstances or downplay events that have transpired in your life; it's an opportunity to consider that there is more than one way to look at situations. It's an opportunity to ease the sting sometimes. To put a little balm on your heart.

Over the years, I discovered the best place to start when I was feeling heavy, blue and out of sorts, was with the things that I normally took for granted.

Here are some examples from my old journals:

I am grateful that my car started this morning.

I am grateful that the light came on when I flicked the switch.

I am grateful for the hot water that came out of the tap.

I am grateful for the extra bag of rice, apple sauce and boxed macaroni and cheese.

My lists would often continue looking like this…

I was grateful for my sweet kitty Luna who, at the time, sat through my tears, anger and frustration at the world. I was grateful for having a roof over my head, even though I was emotionally, mentally, spiritually and financially bankrupt. I was grateful for friends I could connect with honestly. I was grateful for having a job. I was even grateful for the unhealthy relationship at the time because it gave me a distraction and fed right into my codependency journey that I'd not yet healed.

As time went on and the more I healed, my gratitude practice became like air to me. I would cry as I wrote how grateful I was for the money that was coming to me because I'd ironed out my financial ruin. I was grateful for the Creator/Spirit/Universe and the connection I had finally woken up to in myself. I was grateful for the healers, counsellors and therapists that got me to where I was in those days.

Eventually my gratitude practice was slowly finding its way to becoming appreciation for all the things that were seemingly 'not so great.' I became grateful for the struggles, the torment, the agony. The pain. The hardship. The insanity. I became grateful for the life lessons, the bounced payments and the relationships that ended.

I realized that everything had to happen as it did to get me to this point. Here I am today because of all of that, so how could I not be grateful?

Gratitude transformed from being a list I wrote and thoughts I had, to a new lens through which to look at my entire world.

In the space provided, or in your own journal, take a moment to think about a challenge you're currently experiencing. Is there anything within that challenge that you can have some gratitude or appreciation for?

Maybe there's another challenge you had in the past that doesn't leave you feeling so tender now - perhaps there are some things you feel grateful about with that situation.

Has there been a challenge you've had recently that brought you to a new level of awareness or growth?

Maybe you can think of an event or situation that, at first glance, looked like it was not going to turn out well but ended up becoming one of the best things and something you really needed.

CHAPTER FOUR

Gratitude in Motion (On the Go)

Let's kick it up a notch! For this exercise, I invite you to express gratitude on the go or in the moment for everything you touch, see, smell and so on...right in the moment, while you're in motion. Oh, in case you're wondering: yes, you can definitely say these things in your head, but bonus points if you do it out loud and get everyone in the room in on the gratitude vibe!

Examples:

Eyes open – I am so grateful I can see.

First conscious breath – I am so grateful I can breathe.

First moment noticing you are awake – I am so grateful I've been blessed with another day to wake.

When your feet hit the floor, your cozy slippers, the birds you hear out the window, the smell of coffee, the light switches you touch, fresh water, flushing toilet, utensils to cook your breakfast or the money to buy it. Hot, delicious coffee. Your snuggly fur-baby who is looking at you wondering why you ignored them while you slept last night.

You can change your language around this to use words that make sense to you, but the idea is to get into the moment of 'thank you' right here and right now, for all of it.

Some people like to say that they are 'filled with thanks' or 'thank-full' or they just simply say thank you as they go.

Flip on a switch? Thank you.

Car starts? Thank you.

Coffee good? Thank you.

Had a nice conversation with someone? Thank you.

Car doesn't start? Thank you.

Okay, okay, wait a minute. Car not starting? I knew you weren't going to let me get away with this one too easily. Let's talk about that car not starting.

When you learn to appreciate the moments that feel like an annoyance or delay, it may serve you well to recognize that this could be an intentional delay to your timing and could be helping you to avoid an issue you would have been headed into. It could mean avoiding an accident or remembering something you had forgotten to do before you headed off. This is a prime example of gratitude for challenges and irritations. Yes, I know it feels like a stretch, but give it a try next time something feels like a hassle.

CHAPTER FIVE

Prompts and Ideas

Sometimes we can get a little stuck on what to write. Seems odd, but it's true. We are human after all and even the best of intentions can go awry. We can have an exceptionally busy day or perhaps we've had a rotten day and just can't bring ourselves to write anything. Sometimes, we really do want to write and we aren't sure where to start.

Rather than ignoring our practice that day, I like to refer to a little prompt list to help me get into the gratitude groove.

Even if you are totally on point with your gratitude practice, maybe you want to explore some different ideas anyway. Here are a few you can try.

I've broken this down into three parts. People, places and things to get you started. There are plenty of prompts online – but these are some of my favourites.

People

Think of someone who makes your heart sing. Or maybe someone who helped you recently. Who is that special someone you are blessed to have in your life?

Think of someone who helped you in the past but perhaps you didn't have a chance to thank in person. What would you say to them in a letter of gratitude now?

_____
_____
_____
_____
_____
_____
_____
_____
_____
_____
_____
_____
_____
_____

Places

Is there somewhere you love to go and spend time? Maybe it's a special spot in nature or your favourite café. Maybe it's your backyard or a specific place in your home.

A Tiny Book About Gratitude

Things

Do you have something in your life that you just love so much? Maybe it's your favourite blanket, a pen that reminds you of someone or maybe it's your coffee mug or book collection.

CHAPTER SIX

Gratitude – It's in You to Feel

Remember earlier when I mentioned we can sometimes get complacent or feel like the list has become obligatory? This exercise is all about really feeling the gratitude as we are writing the list.

The next time you do your gratitude practice, I invite you to take more time with it. With each item you list, sit with what you've written and feel that appreciation in your heart.

It's great to riddle off a few gratitude comments like coffee and your favourite pen (believe me, I feel both of these in my soul), so do include them…just feel into each of them a little deeper, for a few seconds, with each one you write. Or you could write your list, then read over each item and close your eyes for a moment to really feel them in your heart.

I've often said that it's sometimes hard to explain 'feelings' in words. This is the idea I am going for with this particular exercise. I want you to feel it so deeply that the words escape you or, rather, don't quite measure up to what it is you're truly feeling. So yes, write your list, but also feel your list.

Feel them so deeply you could laugh or cry or squeal with delight and excitement.

Feel them like no one is watching! How absolutely moved or emotionally charged can you let yourself be by experiencing this type of practice fully?

I know this might feel like a stretch, but you've got this. I believe in you.

CHAPTER SEVEN

Gratitude for the Future

Gratitude in advance is an exercise to help you get into the energy and vibe of what you desire in your life. Anything from better communication, health, a home, a vehicle, financial freedom, a good night's sleep tonight… it's all up to you.

When we sit with the Spiritual Laws - in this case, the laws of manifesting and attraction - the only way we can call things into our lives is if we don't feel a sense of 'lacking' them. When we are sitting in the energy of lack, we push things further away from us. Sometimes so far away that they become completely out of reach.

The other thing to keep in mind is that when you write this list, you want to write it in the present tense, as if you already have what you're manifesting. In other words, you should avoid starting your list like this:

'I will be grateful when I…'

The use of 'when I' creates the energy of you not being grateful now which, as I mentioned, pushes the thing away that you're trying to call in.

For example, let's pretend you have back pain. You could write something like 'I am grateful for my healthy and strong back' or 'I am so grateful that my back is flexible and I can move with ease.'

Simply write what you are grateful for, as you would write it like any other gratitude entries you've done so far.

Try to relax into this process. It may feel weird, but trust that your heart will show you where you need to go.

SOME CLOSING THOUGHTS

I hope this book has given you some ideas around starting your gratitude practice or taking it to a new and creative place.

Gratitude is one of the foundational building blocks to designing a life you love. It is often the first thing I need to remind people of when they are feeling down or when they desire a fresh perspective.

I really hope that you take the ideas that resonate the most for you and keep showing up for that idea, day after day.

Gratitude is simple; it just requires a moment of your time. The more moments you give it, the more 'superpower like' it will be.

Your consistency is what contributes to the long-term impact. The day-to-day is great in the moment because you're pausing to be in gratitude.

I often say 'just one moment of gratitude in a day is better than no moments.' Start small, take a tiny step and see where those tiny steps lead you.

It really is a simple practice with superpower strength. It's like a muscle. The more you give it a workout, the strong it will become.

Wishing you gratitude filled days always.

ACKNOWLEDGEMENTS

First and foremost, thank you to you, dear reader, for choosing this book as your next read.

Alexandra Franzen and Lindsey Smith of the Tiny Book Course for helping me learn how to make this all come together, keeping me sane and answering a million questions.

Amanda Gobatto of Digital Girl Consulting, for her friendship and creative talent for marketing, Web Design Work and really, all the things.

Danielle Clarke, for her friendship, editing skills, and cheerleading.

My husband for everything, always.

Pinto, the cat, for walking across the keyboard far too many times.

ABOUT THE AUTHOR

After two decades of working in a typical 9-to-5 corporate environment, Heather decided to make her exit plan and run. She had lived a double life for far too long and finally decided it was time to take her 'secret kitchen table side gig' to the next level and open her healing practice full time as an Intuitive Energy Healer, Medium and Spiritual Guide.

For nearly a decade, she has helped a countless number of people in her healing practice and gets up every day looking forward to meeting whoever she can serve and help next.

She lives with her husband and their fur-kid-cat Pinto in Ontario, Canada.

CONNECTIONS

You can find Heather at www.heathertobin.ca or on social media platforms as @theheathertobin

Remember: if you haven't already joined us online, here's the link to the community to connect with like-souled folks who have a regular daily gratitude practice.

Find us here **www.heathertobin.ca/connection**

ADDITIONAL GRATITUDE PAGES

_____
_____
_____
_____
_____
_____
_____
_____
_____
_____
_____
_____
_____
_____
_____
_____
_____
_____
_____

A Tiny Book About Gratitude

A Tiny Book About Gratitude

A Tiny Book About Gratitude

www.ingramcontent.com/pod-product-compliance
Lightning Source LLC
Chambersburg PA
CBHW020915080526
44589CB00011B/609